ALL THINGS
ANIME AND
MANGA

CULTURAL GUIDE TO ANIME AND MANGA

PAMELA GOSSIN AND MARC HAIRSTON

ReferencePoint
Press

San Diego, CA

About the Authors

Pamela Gossin is a professor of the history of science and literature at the University of Texas at Dallas. Her scholarly research focuses on different forms of literature and science. She and Marc Hairston have cotaught anime and manga classes for college students for over twenty years. Class titles have included Science Fiction and Fantasy, Serious Fun, Apocalypse How?, and Healing Nature. Her favorite anime and manga series is Hayao Miyazaki's *Nausicaä of the Valley of the Wind*, and she still wants to be a princess just like Nausicaä when she grows up.

Marc Hairston is a research space physicist at the University of Texas at Dallas and a lifelong animation fan. As an undergraduate student at Rice University, he split his time between studying literature and physics and started an annual animation festival/party there that is still continuing after forty years. He has published essays and chapters in several academic books about anime as well as in academic journals. But he still does not know how to pilot a Gundam.

For Jack and Aaliyah (so far) and any other grands and great-grands who may join us in this wondrous world.
—PSG

In memory of A. Morales and N. Bahn, two wonderful schoolteachers and Miyazaki fans. We miss them both.
—MRH

© 2024 ReferencePoint Press, Inc.
Printed in the United States

For more information, contact:
ReferencePoint Press, Inc.
PO Box 27779
San Diego, CA 92198
www.ReferencePointPress.com

ALL RIGHTS RESERVED.
No part of this work covered by the copyright hereon may be reproduced or used in any form or by any means—graphic, electronic, or mechanical, including photocopying, recording, taping, web distribution, or Information storage retrieval systems—without the written permission of the publisher.

Picture Credits:
Cover: Al She/Shutterstock.com

6: TCD/Prod.DB/Alamy Stock Photo
10: TCD/Prod.DB/Alamy Stock Photo
12: incamerastock/Alamy Stock Photo
15: NBC/Photofest
17: CPA Media Pte Ltd /Alamy Stock Photo
20: Photo 12/Alamy Stock Photo
23: Photo 12/Alamy Stock Photo
26: Everett Collection Inc/Alamy Stock Photo

29: Album/Alamy Stock Photo
31: Studio Ghibli/BVHE/Photofest
35: Pictures from History/Woodbury & Page/
      Bridgeman Images
38: Cartoon Network/Photofest
41: Studio Ghibli/Disney/Photofest
44: mTaira/Shutterstock
46: Photo 12/Alamy Stock Photo
52: Album/Alamy Stock Photo
54: Studio Ghibli/BVHE/Photofest

LIBRARY OF CONGRESS CATALOGING-IN-PUBLICATION DATA

Names: Gossin, Pamela, author. | Hairston, Marc, author.
Title: Cultural guide to anime and manga / by Pamela Gossin and Marc Hairston.
Description: San Diego, CA : ReferencePoint Press, Inc., 2024. | Series:
    All things anime and manga | Includes bibliographical references and index.
Identifiers: LCCN 2023019045 (print) | LCCN 2023019046 (ebook) | ISBN
    9781678205188 (library binding) | ISBN 9781678205195 (ebook)
Subjects: LCSH: Animated television programs--Japan--Juvenile literature. |
    Animated films--Japan--Juvenile literature. | Manga (Comic
    books)--Juvenile literature. | LCGFT: Television criticism and reviews.
    | Film criticism. | Comics criticism.
Classification: LCC PN1992.8.A59 G67 2024 (print) | LCC PN1992.8.A59
    (ebook) | DDC 791.43/340952--dc23/eng/20230503
LC record available at https://lccn.loc.gov/2023019045
LC ebook record available at https://lccn.loc.gov/2023019046

CONTENTS

INTRODUCTION   4
Cross-Cultural Understanding
Versus Misunderstanding

CHAPTER ONE   8
Art and Other Forms of Visual Storytelling

CHAPTER TWO   16
Historical Eras and Events

CHAPTER THREE   25
Literature

CHAPTER FOUR   33
Folklore, Magic, and Religious and
Spiritual Beliefs

CHAPTER FIVE   42
Nature and Science

CHAPTER SIX   50
Daily Life and Culture

Source Notes   58
For Further Research   60
Anime and Manga Worth Exploring   62
Index   63

INTRODUCTION

CROSS-CULTURAL UNDERSTANDING VERSUS MISUNDERSTANDING

In 2023 fans rushed to see the US premiere of Makoto Shinkai's new film, *Suzume*. Already the fourth-highest-grossing anime film of all time, this fantasy adventure features unusual imagery and plot action inspired by Japanese history, spiritual beliefs, and cultural experiences. Some American viewers—even professional film critics—have difficulty making sense out of what is happening in the film and why. What do those magical doors mean? Why do everyday objects suddenly spring to life? How do an earthquake and tsunami relate to scenes of abandoned buildings and the loss of a parent? Why is a seventeen-year-old girl dealing with all these confusing things?

LAYERS OF MEANING

Like many high-quality anime and manga, this film builds meaning in layers. One layer relates the life and feelings of the main character (who often represents a whole group going through similar things). Others refer to general concerns shared by Japanese people. Still others draw connections to elements of Japan's unique literature, history, and religion. While it is possible to enjoy this fast-paced anime without such information, the more viewers know about Japanese life and culture, the more layers of meaning they can recognize and appreciate.

In 2011 a massive earthquake struck off the northeast coast of Japan, causing extensive damage to towns and villages and to the families who lived in them. People are still recovering from that trauma. Similarly, knowledge of traditional Japanese religious beliefs can help decode the film's visual symbols. In the Shinto religion, doors represent portals between the physical world and the spiritual realm of natural forces. When such gateways open, energy (both creative and destructive) can flow both ways. Shinto also regards living beings and nonliving objects as having souls or spirits, known as kami. So even an old wooden chair can be a companion in a crisis. Cultural references like these help explain the images in this anime as well as Suzume's feelings and actions as a young adult—someone who is just beginning to better understand herself and the world's problems and is still learning what "doors" she must open or close.

Fans who know Shinkai's other works will notice even more clues because he likes to reuse themes, such as climate change, humanity's broken relationship with nature, and the next generation's big challenges to repair and heal the planet. In *Suzume* he is once again telling a story that honors the emotional pain of individuals' loss in the midst of national tragedies and natural disasters. For Shinkai, the personal, the national, and the natural are always interconnected. Regardless of where they live, individuals are connected to each other and to the ecosystems that make up the planet. Surviving and thriving in the future means working together.

FAST FACT

To date, Japanese animators have created over ten thousand separate anime titles (TV series, films, original animations). There are now over ten times that number of published manga titles.

In the new anime film Suzume, *plot and imagery draw on elements of Japanese history, spiritual beliefs, and cultural experiences. As with all anime and manga, the more viewers know about Japanese life and culture, the more layers of meaning they can recognize and appreciate.*

Many anime and manga make their magic by combining references like these. Mamoru Hosoda's *Belle* has many layers of cultural meanings and is inspired by both the classic literary story and the Disney film *Beauty and the Beast*. Like *Suzume*, *Belle* also centers on a teenage girl's personal tragedy. Similarly, Hosoda connects her individual struggles with grief, emotional withdrawal, and learning to use her voice to address larger issues with human disconnection, the lack of caring, and the pros and cons of social media.

As reviewer Justin Chang explains, "It's a tale as old as time and as newfangled as TikTok, in which the virtual world, though packed with fantasy and artifice, can bring startling truths to the surface."[1]

APPRECIATION GROWS THROUGH UNDERSTANDING

Whether we know a little or a lot about Japanese culture, there is no perfect way to arrive at the meaning of any anime or manga. The more references we do understand, however, the more we can enjoy the beauty and creativity of each story. As we learn more about elements that seem mysterious or strange, we discover that we have much in common with the thoughts and feelings of people who live halfway around the world. We also learn there are fun, unexpected, and fascinating differences.

This book is designed to help young American readers understand important aspects of Japanese life and culture as they appear in anime and manga. Japan's culture includes its visual arts and theater, history, literature, folklore, religious and spiritual beliefs, and ideas about the natural world and science, as well as details of everyday people's lives and identities. When we pay close attention to what such cultural references mean and how they are intended, we can avoid confusion and misinterpretations and gain deeper appreciation for others' experiences.

As creative forms of visual storytelling, anime and manga are adding new dimensions to Japanese culture. Fans of anime and manga are part of a growing global youth culture that connects readers and viewers across continents and language groups. Whenever we learn about how Japanese anime creators and manga artists use images and symbols, we are participating in an exciting global community that is building cross-cultural understanding around the world.

This guide explains how major aspects of Japanese culture have influenced important examples of anime and manga. Some titles you may have heard of or seen already. Others may be new and surprising. At the end of the book, we include a list of even more great anime and manga that you may want to explore on your own.

CHAPTER ONE

ART AND OTHER FORMS OF VISUAL STORYTELLING

A single image can tell a whole story. For thousands of years, human beings all over the world have used drawings and paintings to share what they have seen and experienced with others. Many early written languages began as pictograms (picture writing). Japanese artists and storytellers have long combined visual images with verbal narrative to present their stories. Manga and anime are new variations on ancient traditions of visual storytelling. They both draw on the ways that older forms used images, side by side, in sequence to show and tell readers and viewers about the people, places, events, and feelings that happen in their narratives.

EARLY FORMS OF VISUAL STORYTELLING

Before mechanical printing, there were many ways to use visual images in storytelling. During the Middle Ages, some cultures used highly detailed images and designs to illuminate sacred texts like the Bible and Koran. Some decorations were painted right onto the pages to show respect for the meaning and value of the text. During the early 1100s in Japan, a Shinto priest created the famous Bishop Toba Scrolls. Similar to

Aesop's Fables, these told humorous stories about animals, along with ink drawings that showed them doing various human activities. In some ways scroll storytelling is like slow-motion animation because as a scroll unrolls, the images and words appear slowly to the reader's eye, in the order the action occurs. Because of their similarity to comics and simple design, scholars like Frederik L. Schodt consider scrolls to be "among the oldest surviving examples of Japanese narrative comic art."[2]

In the 1300s another classic form of visual storytelling arose in Japan: Noh theater. Originally, these performances took stories from history and mythology and staged them through acting, singing, music, and dance. It was an improvisational, free-form, and experimental way to put on a show that dramatically acted out stories. Key elements of Noh theater are depicted in the anime *Inu-Oh* by Masaaki Yuasa as the performances feature supernatural fantasy elements, demons, and spirits, as well as extreme human emotions, madness, and revenge. Traditional Noh actors wear large, painted wooden masks and elaborate costumes to express the social status and feelings of their characters. Actors use dramatic gestures and deliberate movement instead of a lot of words.

> ## FAST FACT
> Some anime and manga are about people who make anime and manga. *Bakuman* centers on two boys who become manga artists. *Shirabako* follows five high school friends who graduate and start jobs as professional anime voice actors, artists, and production managers.

From the 1600s to the present, Japanese puppet theater (Bunraku) and classical Kabuki dance-dramas continued to develop the visual storytelling methods of Noh theater. Bunraku puppet shows are a popular way to show and tell stories for all ages. Village storytellers attract large audiences and use costumed puppets as actors in classical tales and heroic adventures. Classical Kabuki is famous for attention-grabbing costumes, exaggerated makeup, and its actors' over-the-top emotional expressions. These visual elements combine with narration or dialogue to create entertaining stories about samurai, history, folklore, romance,

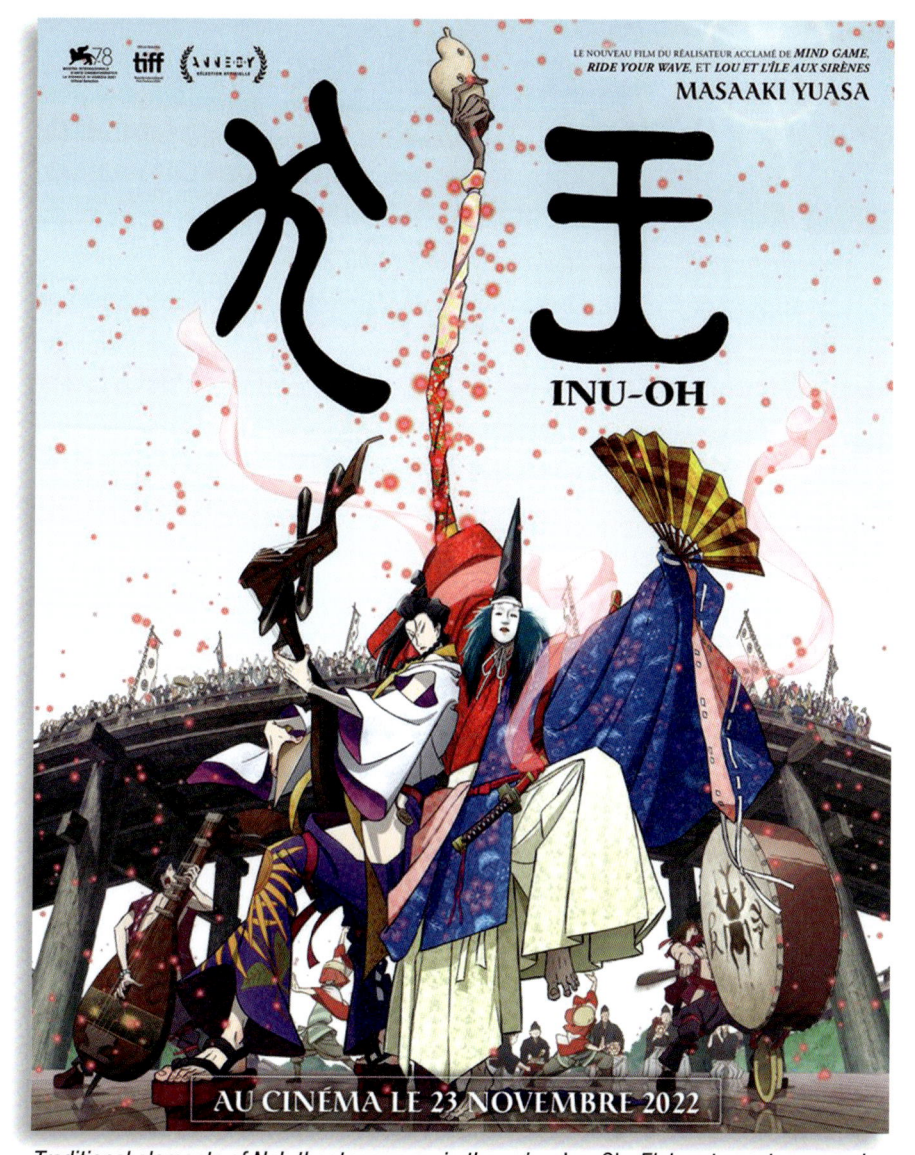

Traditional elements of Noh theater appear in the anime Inu-Oh. *Elaborate costumes and dramatic gestures highlight the supernatural fantasy elements, demons, and spirits, as well as extreme human emotions, madness, and revenge.*

and humor. Favorite scenes from these plays later inspired woodblock prints and illustrated books.

Kabuki performances traditionally focus on moral lessons from the past, supernatural transformations, and human tragedies that cause extreme emotions. One famous element of Kabuki stagecraft is known as *mie*. This refers to a freeze-frame moment when an actor strikes and holds a dramatic pose to emphasize his or her arrival onstage or a signature pose that shows off the actor's costume. When you see anime characters striking such poses (such as Usagi/Sailor Moon after her transformation sequence or any of your favorite *Gundam* robots), this is because the technique adds dramatic effect. It also saves on the number of drawings the animators need to make.

A less well-known form of Japanese visual storytelling is *rakugo*, in which a lone actor kneels on the stage and entertains the audience with a complicated comic tale using wordplay. Such performances began in the mid-1700s and continue to this day. Several anime and manga series feature this unique form of creative storytelling. In *Shōwa Genroku Rakugo Shinjū*, an ex-convict is accepted as an apprentice *rakugo* performer. In the more lighthearted fantasy series *My Master Has No Tail*, a shape-shifting *tanuki* (raccoon-dog) transforms into a human so he can learn how to be a *rakugo* performer.

VISUAL STORYTELLING IN ART AND PAINTING

From the 1600s through the 1800s, an important style of Japanese painting and printmaking was known as *ukiyo-e*, which means "pictures of the floating world." These artists used flat, two-dimensional forms that emphasized large areas of a single color to depict landscapes, everyday life, and people. Perhaps the most famous *ukiyo-e* artist was Katsushika Hokusai, best

KAMISHIBAI

Kamishibai ("paper play") is a traditional form of storytelling in which a street performer recites a story next to a box with a dozen or more painted images that are shown one at a time to accompany the plot. While this practice goes back hundreds of years, it became very popular in Japan during the 1930s and 1940s. The storyteller would gather children around him by selling penny candies and would then perform the story. The storytellers rented printed artwork from publishers so the same fairy tales, adventure stories, and superhero stories could be told all across Japan. After World War II the *kamishibai* practice died out in part because of the rise of manga and television, which was originally called *denki kamishibai* ("electric *kamishibai*") in Japan.

known for *The Great Wave off Kanagawa* (1831). Hokusai and other *ukiyo-e* artists made their livings by producing woodblock images that could be reprinted and sold to the rising middle class. This popular form of art directly influenced the comic book style of manga. In fact, the term *manga* (which means "sketchy" or "whimsical" art) was created about this time to describe this art style. Whenever a single panel of manga or a still image of anime uses simple-shaped areas of a single color to emphasize the flat, two-dimensional nature of the cartoon world (like in *Pokémon*), it is directly reflecting this nineteenth-century style.

Traditional Japanese watercolor painting often uses skilled brushstrokes to imply the general shapes of objects, so viewers must fill in the gaps of the artwork with their own minds and imaginations. This style aims to give the impression of an object, not depict it with exact realism as in traditional European art. In the mid-1800s this form of Japanese painting inspired famous European

The art form known as ukiyo-e, *a style of Japanese woodblock painting and printmaking, directly influenced the comic book style of manga. Pictured is Katsushika Hokusai's famous 1831 woodblock print,* The Great Wave off Kanagawa.

artists such as Monet, Renoir, and van Gogh to start what is now called the impressionist movement. Both manga and anime have been influenced by this style. Isao Takahata's *The Tale of the Princess Kaguya* (2013) was intentionally designed to look like an animated watercolor painting. To achieve that magical effect, artists used newly developed computer graphics to generate and manipulate tens of thousands of individual watercolor images of the characters and action until they appeared truly fluid in motion.

> **FAST FACT**
>
> Anime storytelling has taken many forms. The Royal Shakespeare Company in London, England, created a stage production of *My Neighbour Totoro* in 2022 that used giant puppets for Totoro and Catbus.

NEW FORMS OF VISUAL STORYTELLING: MANGA AND ANIME

Although even one still image or a single dramatic stage scene can tell a captivating story, multiple images used in sequence can build more complex worlds and narratives. While historical forms of Japanese visual art were referred to as manga, what we now think of as manga comics truly began in the late 1800s. This development was inspired in part by imported British and French caricature cartoons. In the early 1900s, stories presented by illustrated panels with text balloons began to appear in Japanese newspapers and children's magazines. After World War II, economic poverty limited much of the Japanese public to inexpensive forms of entertainment. Magazines with manga stories and serials published on cheap newsprint were easily affordable, and they became so popular in the late 1940s and 1950s that they spawned a boom in modern manga publishing.

The central figure in this boom was artist Osamu Tezuka, whom anime scholar Helen McCarthy calls "a medium shaper, the chief architect of the modern anime and manga industries."[3] Trained as a doctor, Tezuka's true passions were drawings and movies. After the war he found great success drawing motion-picture-style manga serials for several different magazines. His works became so popular that when other magazines could not hire him, they

13

FAST FACT

In 1965, when Stanley Kubrick began making his epic science fiction movie, *2001: A Space Odyssey*, he wanted someone with a futuristic vision as his art designer. The first person Kubrick asked was Osamu Tezuka, but he was too busy and turned Kubrick down.

hired other artists and asked them to make something like Tezuka's manga. Over his career Tezuka produced over 700 volumes of manga totaling over 150,000 pages. In the 1960s he founded one of the first animation companies in Japan, Mushi Production, and began making anime based on his work. In the United States he is best known for the anime shows *Astro Boy* and *Kimba the White Lion*. Tezuka's innovative drawing style heavily influenced every manga and anime artist who came after him. Renowned animator and director Hayao Miyazaki famously complained that his early artwork looked so much like Tezuka's that he had to struggle hard to break free of his influence.

Anime and manga are both influenced by elements of traditional Japanese visual and performing art forms. Both combine images and words that are read or viewed in sequence. Like Tezuka, many manga artists also create anime. Indeed, today most anime series are based on preexisting popular manga serials. This makes sense economically, because manga are much cheaper to create than animated films. As a result, thousands of manga are published each year, so anime producers usually adapt the best

MISS HOKUSAI *AND HER FATHER*

The anime film *Miss Hokusai* is a fictionalized biography of the life of Oi Katsushika, the daughter of the famous *ukiyo-e* artist Katsushika Hokusai, who created *The Great Wave off Kanagawa*. Oi was an artist in her own right, but only ten artworks still exist that we know for certain were created by her alone. During her father's later years, she helped him with his work as he became increasingly disabled. Since Hokusai was the famous master who oversaw the production of the artwork, little or no credit was given to any of his assistants.

Proving how much of his work came from Oi can only be argued with circumstantial evidence. Critics have noted some stylistic changes in his later works that may show her influence. In an online post, anime scholar Jonathan Clements proposes that one of Hokusai's last works, *Tiger in the Snow*, is most likely a work by Oi rather than her father. The anime film dramatically depicts the creative tension between daughter and father, as well as the ongoing financial struggle they both experienced trying to make their living as artists during this period.

The work of the prolific manga artist Osamu Tezuka shaped the modern manga and anime industries. Tezuka is best known in the United States for Astro Boy *(pictured), a television anime show that first ran in the 1960s.*

sellers, knowing that there is a built-in viewing (and buying) audience just waiting for the TV series or film to premiere.

BACK TO THE FUTURE

In an interesting twist, popular stories from manga and anime are now being adapted back into Japanese theater. This began in the 1960s, when theatrical groups began producing action-packed, special effects shows and musicals they called Super Kabuki. This styling was perfect for adapting anime and manga shows in the 1970s, when the Takarazuka Revue staged *The Rose of Versailles*. Since then various stage productions of *Sailor Moon, Naruto, One Piece, InuYasha*, and *Mobile Suit Gundam 00* have been produced. These shows feature anime-style visuals; fast-paced, action-packed choreography; stunts; and special effects. The popularity of these productions has revived profits for the traditional stage and raised fans' interest in theater. This crossover makes sense because, as writer Kayson Carlin says, "both are mediums used by storytellers to invite others into another world."[4] Working together, old and new forms of visual storytelling connect Japan's past to the present and bring anime and manga characters to life.

CHAPTER TWO

HISTORICAL ERAS AND EVENTS

Taylor Swift's Eras Tour celebrated the albums she has created through different stages of her career. Teens' personal eras mark turning points in their relationships and emotions as well as tastes in food, music, and fashion. For historians, however, *historical eras* refer to seriously long time periods during which cultures undergo major changes.

Three main time periods shape Japanese history: the early era, from the beginning to about 710 CE; the classical era, from 710 to 1854 CE; and the modern era, from 1854 CE to the present. The early era records Japan's origin stories. The classical era is a period of power struggles over natural resources and between ruling families. The modern era records dramatic shifts in Japanese society and technology. Events from all of these eras influence Japan's rich storytelling traditions in both old and new media. As Japanese comics scholar Frederik L. Schodt states, anime and manga now have "as much to say about life as novels or films."[5]

All human stories are based on history, even if they imagine fictional futures or alternative histories. Relatively new as forms of visual narrative, anime and manga still draw on ancient myths and legends as well as actual events from Japan's past.

THE EARLY ERA: MYTHIC ORIGINS

Few reliable records document Japan's early era. Myths and legends about it, though, inspire many images, symbols, and characters in anime and manga. Allusions to early Japanese myths are instantly recognized by home audiences, yet they often blow right past viewers from outside Japan.

One early creation myth tells how the god Izanagi and the goddess Izanami formed the islands of Japan and gave birth to other deities, including the sun goddess, Amaterasu; the moon god, Tsukuyomi; and the storm god, Susanoo. When the storm god wreaked havoc on the world, it frightened Amaterasu so much that she hid in a cave. The loss of her sunlight then caused more disasters, so all the spirits tried to coax her out of hiding. Their solution was to hold a wild party outside her cave. When

Light and warmth are restored in the world after the frightened sun goddess Amaterasu peeks out of her cave hiding place. Manga and anime artists have used imagery from this creation myth in their work.

> **FAST FACT**
>
> In *Sailor Moon*, the talismans of the three outer *senshi* (guardians) are references to the three sacred treasures of Amaterasu: the Space Sword, the Deep Aqua Mirror, and the Garnet Orb.

Amaterasu could not resist peeking out to see what was going on, they pulled her out to restore her light and warmth to the world.

This myth has been used to explain why Japan identifies as the "land of the rising sun" and why images like the red circle appear on the flag and are so ubiquitous in Japanese art. The glowing sun represents cycles of creation and destruction, or birth and rebirth. It also symbolizes apocalyptic change, such as that caused by the sunlike fireball of an atomic bomb. Such imagery appears in both Osamu Tezuka's original 1949 manga, *Metropolis*, and director Rintaro's retro-futuristic 2001 anime adaptation of it.

This mythology also helped establish the belief that emperors were descended from the gods, specifically the sun goddess herself. As evidence of their divine status, they claim to have inherited three sacred treasures from her: a mirror and a jewel used to draw her out of her cave and a dragon's sword.

Anime references to this myth and these sacred items are not always serious or reverent. In *Kannagi*, the temple kami, Nagi, acting like a bratty Amaterasu, gets upset and pouts in a closet. When she refuses to budge, her twin sister kami, Zange, tries to tempt her out through jealousy by holding a party in the room and pretending to make out with Nagi's love interest.

THE EARLY ERA: JAPAN'S DISTANT PAST

Most historians and anthropologists believe that the islands of Japan were first populated by indigenous peoples known as the Emishi and Ainu. Such groups established the Shinto religion, which includes the belief that kami inhabit everything that exists, including all living and nonliving objects and natural places.

In Hayao Miyazaki's *Princess Mononoke*, Shinto ideas are portrayed through the culture of one of the main characters, Ashitaka, and his village's spiritual beliefs as well as the depiction of animals as sentient gods, and the adorable *kodama* (tree spirits) that fill the deer-like god Nightwalker's forest. Shinto references also appear in two more of Miyazaki's films, *Spirited Away* and *My Neighbor Totoro*. According to anime scholar Susan Napier, both anime convey that "belief in the powers of nature and the imagination will give us the strength to go beyond ourselves and transcend the traumas of daily life."[6]

Anime and manga set in recent times also depict ancient Shinto beliefs, temples, shrines, and rituals as a way to show that Japanese people are still connected to their distant past. The lighthearted TV series *Kamichu!* features many cute moments as the middle school main character (a goddess herself) interacts with the myriad kami she sees all around her. Some are the spirits of CDs, laser discs, and tofu. Others are her three goofy spirit animals—a boar, deer and butterfly, whose Japanese names Ino, Shika, Chou indicate a winning combination in the card game *hanafuda*. As noted by anime scholar Antonia Levi, "The Shinto ability to blend the fantastic with the everyday is basic to Japanese life and the world of anime. . . . It is also one of the features that makes anime so attractive to young Americans, especially those interested in alternate forms of spirituality."[7]

WHAT IS A SAMURAI?

The samurai were the professional warrior class of Japanese society. They started as an outer circle of aristocrats who served as soldiers to protect the emperor during the Nara and Heian periods (710–1192 CE). Their code of conduct prized honesty, benevolence, and self-sacrifice. They swore loyalty to the emperor and later to other ruling families. Samurai often fought battles against other samurai, but despite their origins as warriors, they also became the driving force behind many of the Japanese cultural arts. Samurai were not only valued as fighters but were expected to be poets and appreciators of tea ceremonies and Noh theater.

Tales of samurai and their exploits are common subjects of anime series such as *Samurai X* or *The Dagger of Kamui*. Giant robot (or mecha) series have their origins in samurai dramas, with the pilots of the mecha exhibiting samurai values and a warrior's sense of honor. The giant robots themselves, especially in *Gundam*, are deliberately designed to look like samurai armor. In US popular culture, the Jedi Order in the *Star Wars* franchise is based on the samurai, with Darth Vader's armor, particularly his helmet, specifically copied from that worn by samurai Date Masamune, who lived from 1567 to 1636.

CLASSICAL ERA INSPIRATIONS

Japan's classical era is best known for the historical battles of its emperors, shoguns, and samurai warriors. The period was also famous for its creative cultural achievements. During this time, several forms of Buddhism were imported from China, and classical Japanese painting, poetry, music, and theater were developed and refined.

Today there are almost as many samurai and ninja anime and manga (*Ninja Scroll*, *Samurai X*, *The Dagger of Kamui*, to name a few) as there were actual samurai and ninja. Anime featuring giant battling robots, including *Gundam*, and the robots' styling directly reflect historic samurai warriors and their unique ethic. The horned helmets and armor of the *Gundam* robots reflect the designs of classic samurai armor, while the conflicts and battles they fight embody important samurai ethics like courage, respect, and justice.

Anime and manga inspired by the classical era also relate other kinds of human "battles." In *The Tale of the Princess Kaguya*, Isao Takahata adapts an old folktale about a poor bamboo cutter

The Tale of Princess Kaguya *(pictured) is based on a folktale about a poor bamboo cutter who finds a magical baby with celestial origins. The film adapts and blends classical Japanese scroll painting with computer-assisted, watercolor freehand animation.*

who finds a magical baby with celestial origins. The film depicts the struggles that often arise between traditional expectations of families and society and the new hopes and dreams of the next generation. To show that such creative conflicts need not end with one destroying the other, Takahata honors both old and new ideas by adapting and blending the classical style of Japanese scroll painting into his modern computer-assisted, watercolor freehand animation.

Classical era anime also portray how humans struggle with their creative and destructive sides. *The Heike Story* retells a classic Japanese tale about the Genpei War (1180–1185), during which two rival clans, the Taira and Minamoto (aka the Heike and Genji) try to destroy each other. As a result, their cultures now only exist in the stories told about them. Presented from the artistic perspective of a young girl who plays the *biwa*, an ancient musical instrument, and can foretell the future, the series expresses how creativity triumphs over pointless destruction.

> ### *FAST FACT*
> In the classical era, being true samurai meant being warriors and fighters who also wrote poetry, held tea ceremonies, and did flower arranging (ikebana). These activities were believed to focus the mind and calm the soul.

Important contributions of artistic expression during the classical era are also reflected in Masaaki Yuasa's film, *Inu-Oh*. When classical Noh theater was first founded in the 1300s, creativity and free expression clashed with established forms of political and social control. The main characters in this story, a blind biwa player and a physically disabled actor, represent how the socially marginalized creatives of the time struggled with poverty and prejudice. As an artistic team, they collaboratively invent a new form of music and dance (think TikTok) that captivates popular audiences. When the crowds go wild, it greatly offends court authorities, who try to shut down the fun. The film's "blast from the past" life lesson is reinforced by its rock music soundtrack to make it loud and clear that inclusion and creative freedom can unite society better than outdated rules and restrictions.

HOW MANY KAMI ARE THERE?

Kami are the gods or the divine spirits in the Shinto religion in Japan. Shinto is a pantheistic religion that considers all material objects and places to be inhabited by kami. If you ask a Japanese person how many kami there are, they will likely say 8 million, which does not mean that is the exact number—it just means there are so many it is beyond counting. The sun goddess Amaterasu is considered the first and primary Shinto kami, followed by the other characters in the creation story and on down to the local kami for each mountain, valley, river, body of water, storm, wind, thunder, fishing, and so on. In the film *Spirited Away*, Haku is the kami for a small river that has been paved over and so has lost his memory. The manga and anime series *Otaku Elf* tells the comic story of a modern Shinto shrine whose kami is actually a six-hundred-year-old elf, who is a shut-in obsessed with anime and video games, and Koito, the high school girl and *miko* (shrine maiden) who has to deal with this dysfunctional deity.

THE MODERN ERA

For centuries Japan closed itself off from the outside world. In 1854 Japan signed a treaty with the United States allowing trade between the two countries. At the same time, Japan began to modernize its schools, agriculture, and industries by importing and adapting European and American ideas and practices. By the 1920s it had become the premier industrial nation in Asia. After its military involvement in World War II resulted in social and economic disaster, Japan refocused its national priorities and became a world leader in high-tech electronics and entertainment.

Most anime and manga today are set in the modern era, so it is no surprise that they feature stories about how regular Japanese people live their lives. *Sazae-San*, the longest-running animated series of all time, portrays daily events in a middle-class Japanese family after World War II. Originally created in 1969, it is still going strong. *My Neighbors the Yamadas*, a comedy-drama anime, also offers a slice of modern life as it

FAST FACT

When Japan reformed its school system in the late 1800s, administrators copied the curriculum of European schools and modeled their uniforms after modern European sailors. Japanese school uniforms are still called sailor suits, and girls typically wear sailor-style blouses and skirts with a ribbon or bow.

relates the imperfect but loving interrelationships in one extended Japanese family.

Other modern stories focus on the challenges Japanese people have experienced as aspects of their culture shifted from traditional to more contemporary lifestyles. Two intriguing anime that reflect these changes are *Spring and Chaos* and *The Life of Budori Gusuko*, which are both inspired by the real life and ideas of poet, novelist, and agronomist Kenji Miyazawa. These films relate how rural folks were caught between old farming traditions and modern scientific agriculture as they struggled to grow crops and feed their families. Which are better: the new techniques or what their grandparents taught them? Similar tensions between old and new are represented in the TV series *Samurai Champloo*.

The shift from a traditional way of life to a more contemporary lifestyle has posed challenges for the Japanese people. The tensions between old and new appear in anime such as The Life of Budori Gusuko *(pictured).*

These stories dramatically contrast their historical setting, a time and place of strict social conformity, with the relatable adventures and modern personalities of three counterculture characters: a tea waitress, outlaw, and ronin (masterless samurai). The show's contemporary message of tolerance for minorities and marginalized groups is further symbolized by its unexpected hip-hop soundtrack.

HISTORY LESSONS

Learning from history is something we all do as individuals and as societies. Telling stories about the past helps us understand, honor, and remember what is most beautiful and important. Such stories also remind us about the kinds of human choices we need to change and never repeat. Satoshi Kon's *Millennium Actress* shows how one person's life is connected to national and global events. The title character's roles span more than a thousand years of Japanese history. As the film recaps her acting career, it unrolls like a historical scroll that shows key moments from the classical era all the way into the twenty-first century. In the end, she learns (as viewers do) that every era has something valuable to teach us.

CHAPTER THREE

LITERATURE

No story is ever 100 percent new and original in every aspect. All writers draw from works they have seen, heard, or read. The creators of anime are no exception. Anime borrows from the rich heritage of Japanese literature as well as the literature of other cultures. The very first feature-length color animated film ever produced in Japan was *Legend of the White Serpent* (1957), and it was based on a classic Chinese folktale of a young man who falls in love with a snake that can transform itself into a beautiful young woman.

CLASSICAL ASIAN AND JAPANESE LITERATURE

A famous classic work of Chinese literature, *Journey to the West* (*The Monkey King*), has influenced numerous anime and manga. In this tale, Sun Wokong, the Monkey King, invades Chinese heaven, the home of Chinese ancestors and deities, because he considers himself their equal. At first, the Jade Emperor, leader of the deities, allows him to stay and gives him a formal position. But when Sun tries to steal the sacred peaches of immortality, he is trapped by the divine Buddha (the founder of the Buddhist religion in India) and forced to return to Earth. To atone for his crime, the Monkey King must guide and protect a Chinese monk on his quest to India to bring back Buddhist scriptures. Framed as a religious pilgrimage, the story mostly focuses on the adventures that occur during this road trip.

In the mid-twentieth century, Osamu Tezuka published a manga serial for children based on this story, entitled *My Songuku*. (Son Guku is the Japanese version of the Monkey King's name). Later adapted as an anime, *Journey to the West*, it was released in the United States as *Alakazam the Great*. Like the original, in Tezuka's versions the main character is a clever, disobedient monkey who offends the gods by stealing forbidden fruit. During the long trek to make amends, he and his companions must overcome many challenges, deserts, mountains, and volcanoes, as well as dangerous encounters with magical creatures.

In 1984 Akira Toriyama created a manga series based on *Journey to the West*. Later adapted into two anime series, *Dragonball* and *Dragonball Z*, these stories center on Goku—a thrill-seeking warrior who possesses a magical Power Pole and Flying Nimbus. Both of these devices are direct references to the Monkey King's magical staff and flying cloud. The seven dragon balls that Goku seeks represent the original quest for the Buddhist sutras (holy scriptures). These journeys are now some of the most popular anime worldwide. Rivaling the massive length of the Chinese

Son Goku, the Monkey King, is depicted with his magical staff and flying cloud in this nineteenth-century woodcut by a Japanese artist. Imagery from this tale appears in manga by Osamu Tezuka and in the Dragonball *and* Dragonball Z *stories.*

tale, the series now has over three hundred episodes and has inspired the creation of other hugely popular anime series such as *One Piece*, *Fairy Tail*, *Bleach*, and *Naruto*, as well as related video games and live-action musicals.

Storylines and characters from classical Japanese stories and classical Western literature have also been adapted into anime and manga. The main character of Hayao Miyazaki's epic manga, *Nausicaä of the Valley of the Wind*, was equally inspired by a minor character of the same name in Homer's Greek epic poem *The Odyssey* and the heroine of the twelfth-century Japanese tale "The Princess That Loved Insects" (author unknown). In both stories, the strong young female character possesses unusual intelligence, is curious about nature, and shows empathy for all livings things. As Miyazaki says, "Unconsciously, Nausicaä and this Japanese princess became one person in my mind."[8] In Miyazaki's manga and anime, his flying girl Nausicaä is a scientist-heroine who loves insects and saves her male mentor, then saves her village, her allies and enemies, and ultimately the whole world.

> ### FAST FACT
> Kenji Miyazawa's famous poem "The Morning of the Last Farewell" describes the final moments when his younger sister died of tuberculosis. These mournful verses are used in the anime *The Place Promised in Our Early Days* and in two series, *O Maidens in Your Savage Season* and *Beyond the Boundary*.

JAPANESE FANTASY AND SCIENCE FICTION LITERATURE

While most anime are based on manga or games, many are inspired by Japanese fantasy and science fiction. Kenji Miyazawa was a writer who lived in the early 1900s and died at age thirty-seven. Though he was unknown during his lifetime, his friends later promoted his works. His children's fantasy novella, *Night on the Galactic Railroad*, is now famous and widely read in Japanese schools. The story begins on the night of a summer festival when two friends—Giovanni and Campanella—board a dreamlike train that takes them through the stars. It turns out that they are traveling through various kinds of heavenly afterlives. At the end, when Giovanni returns to the festival alone, he learns that Campanella had been riding the train to arrive

"GRAVE OF THE FIREFLIES"

In 1967 Akiyuki Nosaka wrote a partly autobiographical short story, "Grave of the Fireflies," about two children—an older brother named Seita and his preschool-aged sister, Setsuko—who starve to death during the closing days of World War II. In real life, Nosaka survived the war but lost his sister. He wrote the story as an apology to her, and it became a critical success. Japanese schools made it required reading for middle and high school students, much like *The Diary of Anne Frank* is used in US schools, to show the inhumanity of war.

The publishing company hired Studio Ghibli and director Isao Takahata to make an anime feature based on the story, and the film version was released in Japan in 1988. Takahata was himself a survivor of the wartime bombing, and he felt a deep kinship with the story and saw deep lessons in it. According to film scholar Alex Dudok de Wit, Takahata "believed that young people [of the 1980s boom], pampered by consumerism, were losing their sense of social responsibility. Strikingly, he saw parallels between this problem and the fate of Seita and Setsuko."

Alex Dudok de Wit, *Grave of the Fireflies*. London: Bloomsbury, 2021, p. 14.

at his idea of heaven because he drowned while trying to save another student. This tenderhearted story helps children understand important ideas about life and death, friendship, self-sacrifice, and the meaning of true happiness.

In 1985 an anime based on this story was made using cats that walk and talk like humans for the characters. The creators made that unusual choice because they realized that the story had so captured the imaginations of thousands of Japanese children that they feared their character designs could never compete with how all those young readers envisioned them. To avoid disappointing their audience, they substituted cats instead. As in the original, the anime gently conveys its message of universal love and acceptance against the background of the Milky Way.

Science fiction from the literary world has inspired other anime as well. Two works by popular science fiction writer Yasutaka Tsutsui have been turned into high-profile anime films. In his story, *The Girl Who Leapt Through Time*, Tsutsui explores what happens when Kazuko, a high school girl, discovers that she can leap backward in time to correct mistakes she has made. She soon learns that this ability comes with a heavy price. This novella was made into a live-action TV series. Later, in an anime feature film, director Mamoru Hosada further expanded the story by imagining that Kazuko's niece, Makoto, also has time-leaping talent. Hosoda's version of *The Girl Who Leapt Through Time* won the 2007 Japanese Academy Award for best animated feature.

Tsutsui also wrote a science fiction thriller, *Paprika*, about a psychiatrist, Dr. Atsuko Chiba, who developed an electronic device that allows her to enter other people's dreams while they sleep. Atsuko and her dream-state persona, Paprika, intend to use this device as therapy for psychiatric patients. However, when it is stolen and misused, they must find a way to stop the dream world from taking over reality. Satoshi Kon's full-length anime adaptation of the same name closely follows the themes and characters used in the 1993 novel. The film, released in 2006, features Kon's trademark style of brightly colored, surreal imagery, in which creepy oversized dolls, puppets, and masked characters escape dreams and trespass into reality. The storyline and unusual visual elements likely influenced the 2010 US film *Inception*.

An anime adaptation of the science fiction novel Paprika *features filmmaker Satoshi Kon's trademark style. As seen here, this style includes brightly colored, surreal imagery where creepy oversized dolls and puppets escape dreams and trespass into reality.*

A FAVORITE BOOK FROM CHILDHOOD

All types of literature have inspired anime and manga creators. Hayao Miyazaki's newest anime film, scheduled to premiere in Japan in July 2023, is based on one of his favorite books from his childhood. The 1937 novel *How Do You Live?* by Genzaburo Yoshino tells the story of fifteen-year-old Junichi Honda (nicknamed Koperu, after Copernicus) as he struggles to understand the meaning of life and his place in the world. The film's producer, Toshio Suzuki, says that Miyazaki's film does not stick literally to the novel's plot but instead creates a "fantasy on a grand scale" inspired by it. When asked if he has the answer to the question in the film's title, Miyazaki replied, "I am making this movie because I do not have the answer."

Quoted in Ligaya Mishan, "Hayao Miyazaki Prepares to Cast One Last Spell," *New York Times*, November 23, 2021. www.nytimes.com.

LITERARY FICTION

Not all uses of literature in anime and manga are full adaptations. Brief allusions and references to literary works are also frequent. Kafka Asagiri's manga series, *Bungo Stray Dogs* (also an anime series and movie), relates the stories of young detectives who take on the names and personas of famous Japanese authors, including mystery writer Edogawa Ranpo and fantasy writer Kenji Miyazawa. Other characters are named after (and act like) famous writers of world literature, such as the American Mark Twain (best known for *Huckleberry Finn* and *Tom Sawyer*) and Irishman Bram Stoker, author of *Dracula*.

A fascinating crossover between well-known modern Japanese fiction and anime can be found in Yoshitoshi ABe's TV series *Haibane-Renmei*. Over thirteen episodes, ABe (who blends his original pen name, AB, with his surname, Abe) creates a story about a dreamlike afterlife in a walled city inhabited by gray-winged children. The setting for this anime and many of its visual symbols were inspired by Haruki Murakami's novel *Hard-Boiled Wonderland and the End of the World*. Half of this complex book takes place in a strange walled city with a library and a deeply mysterious forest, where only crows can fly out and wells carry water and shadows away. For most of the plot, the main character tries to figure out why he is there and whether he should stay or try to escape. As ABe confesses, "[That] is my favorite book, and I've already read it more than 10 times. . . . I was thinking of the novel when I made . . . each episode's title [in] three phrases, as well as the birds, the well, the wall, the inviolable forest and the library." Although these specific images do mirror Murakami's, ABe uses them to create a completely different story, and he cautions American fans to not take the similarities too literally. The *hai* in the title word *haibane* means "ash gray," indicating that ABe's anime has ambiguous gray areas. As he puts it, "It is not a story to find answers, but [one] to wonder about the answers."[9]

CROSS-CULTURAL INFLUENCES OF WORLD LITERATURE

In general, Japanese readers are more familiar with Western literature than American students are with Asian stories. Anime, then, often draw on Japanese audiences' favorite works of Western literature. Miyazaki and Studio Ghibli are particularly noted for this. In *Castle in the Sky*, the floating castle, Laputa, is named after the fictitious floating island inhabited by mad scientists in Jonathan Swift's *Gulliver's*

The floating castle (pictured) in Castle in the Sky *was inspired by the floating island in Jonathan Swift's* Gulliver's Travels. *Many anime draw on favorite works of Western literature.*

FAST FACT

A Möbius strip is piece of paper that looks like it has two sides, but really only has one side. Japanese and American popular culture may look like two different things, but they really are part of one continuous pop culture.

Travels. The plot and characters of *Howl's Moving Castle* are closely based on British fantasy writer Diana Wynne Jones's young adult novel of the same name. *The Secret World of Arrietty* beautifully illustrates the visual details and family spirit of the "little" world depicted in English writer Mary Norton's book *The Borrowers*—miniature furniture, spools of thread, and all.

Some anime and manga adaptations of European classics stay truer to the originals than others. Hideaki Anno's beautifully crafted 1990 series *Nadia—the Secret of Blue Water* was inspired by Jules Verne's science fiction adventure novel, *20,000 Leagues Under the Sea*. In Anno's series, fourteen-year-old Nadia and a young French inventor, Jean, join forces with Captain Nemo on his famous submarine to save the world from evil forces. In a similar way, the anime *Gankutsuou* reimagines *The Count of Monte Cristo*, a historical revenge novel by Alexandre Dumas (the author of the swashbuckling *Three Musketeers*), by setting it in outer space, thousands of years in the future.

Since opening up to the world nearly two hundred years ago, Japanese culture has eagerly collected, learned from, and sought to learn more about world literature. These works are now an integral part of Japanese culture. Beginning in 1969 a weekly animated series now known as *World Masterpiece Theater* introduced Japanese children to classic literature from outside Japan. These shows were extremely popular with both children and adults for nearly thirty years. Some of the best-loved series were based on European and American stories, including *Lassie*, *Little Women*, *Anne of Green Gables*, and *Heidi, Girl of the Alps*.

World cultures are forever loaning and borrowing literary stories and ideas from each other. Scholar of Japanese culture Roland Kelts describes this constant global exchange as the "'Möbius strip' of interrelations between Japanese and American artists—a cross-pollination of influences."[10] Cultural and literary inspirations constantly flow around the world, enrich us, and connect us to each other.

CHAPTER FOUR

FOLKLORE, MAGIC, AND RELIGIOUS AND SPIRITUAL BELIEFS

Weird things happen in the world. Every culture invents stories about the invisible forces and unexplained phenomena that humans encounter in their lives and nature. Folklore beliefs are passed down as fairy tales, nursery rhymes, songs, legends, and superstitions. Magical beliefs involve ideas about how to control the supernatural through spells and curses. Religious and spiritual beliefs offer explanations about good and evil and the gods or spirits that manifest them. Anime and manga are new forms of folklore that combine traditional and modern beliefs about the unknown.

INSPIRATIONS FROM FOLKLORE

Japan's supernatural creatures are not the same as Anglo-European ones. *Yokai* is sometimes translated as "demon," but they are more like spirits or imps and are rarely evil. *Akuma* are similar to Western-style evil demons, while *oni* are violent, ogre-type villains who wear tiger-skin clothing. In the series *Urusei Yatsura*, Lum, the alien teenaged girl, is a comic version of an *oni*, which explains her short temper and tiger-skinned bikini. Part of the fun of anime and manga is meeting the unusual mythical beings in them.

FAST FACT

In *The Melancholy of Haruhi Suzumiya*, teen Haruhi is actually a god, but she does not realize it. Her unusual friends (including a space alien and a time traveler) must work tirelessly to amuse and distract her so she does not accidentally destroy the universe with divine emotional outbursts: a typical day for a high school diva.

In Japanese folklore, *tanuki* (raccoon-dogs) and foxes are shape-shifters and tricksters who pester humans. In Isao Takahata's anime *Pom Poko*, their annoying characteristics are used to satirize 1960s student protests against the US and Japanese governments and the Vietnam War. When their forest is about to be bulldozed for new housing, the tanuki take on human and supernatural forms to scare off the developers and new residents. When their sabotage fails, some remain as humans trying to blend in, while others move onto the golf course that used to be their forest. In *Our Home's Fox Deity* (light novel, anime), two teenaged brothers return to their late mother's home to find themselves subject to accidents and curses caused by yokai. A fox spirit who has guarded the family for generations arrives to protect them. Appearing as a fox or human as need arises, her clever powers can defeat any enemy, but she struggles to adapt to modern ways. The clash of traditional nature spirits with contemporary environments represents similar struggles to adapt that many Japanese people have experienced over the years.

Stories of adaptation and survival are also featured in *Demon Slayer*. A young boy, Tanjiro Kamado, lives in the mountains of Japan in the early 1900s and cares for his siblings after their father dies. When demons attack, his sister is turned into a half human/half demon. In order to restore her, Tanjiro trains as a demon slayer and fights many battles to find a cure. Tales of yokai-inflicted trauma and conflict are also featured in *In/Spectre*. When she was a child, the yokai took college student Kotoko's right eye and left leg in exchange for making her their goddess of wisdom who settles their disputes and solves their mysteries. She is assisted by another student who ate the flesh of two different yokai as a child and is now immortal with the gift of precognition. Both narratives serve as modern folktales to illustrate that unfortunate things happen and that life involves loss and compromise, so we must battle to survive.

Many of the demons in Demon Slayer *come from Japanese folklore. Like the mythological yokai* Tsuchigumo *(pictured), the Father Spider Demon in* Demon Slayer *can shed a layer of his skin and grow to an enormous size.*

THE MAGIC OF WITCHES AND WIZARDS

Witches do not exist within traditional Japanese folklore or beliefs. The idea for them was borrowed from Western stories about witches and other magic users, but it is now a key feature of Japanese popular culture. Hayao Miyazaki's *Howl's Moving Castle* tells of Sophie, a young woman turned into an old woman by a witch, her relationship with the vain wizard Howl, and how they redeem each other from curses. In *Kiki's Delivery Service*, a thirteen-year-old witch leaves home to begin her magical apprenticeship, similar to Japanese teens who leave home for boarding school to start new lives in new communities. In other young witch anime, teens attend a school for magic like Hogwarts in the *Harry Potter* series. In *Little Witch Academia*, a young girl with no magical background follows her idol to enroll in Luna Nova Magical Academy. Once there, she discovers a mysterious wand and develops her own magical talents.

Stories about learning magical skills and magic gone wild both reflect typical growing-up experiences as young adults become aware of their capabilities and test out their personal capabilities. The manga series *Witch Hat Atelier* was chosen as one of the ten best graphic novels for teens by the American Library Association in 2020. The story is set in a world where spells are cast by writing magical script with enchanted ink. The central character, a young girl named Coco, accidentally casts a spell and becomes apprenticed to a male witch. As she and others practice their craft, they must navigate the intrigues and infighting of the Witches Assembly. The series *The Familiar of Zero* plays the magical academy idea for laughs. The protagonist is a noblewoman who has zero magical talent; hence her nickname, Louise the Zero. When students first cast a spell to call their familiar, most produce the

CHRISTIANITY AND JUDAISM IN NEON GENESIS EVANGELION

Christianity first came to Japan with Catholic missionaries in the 1500s. Periodically banned through the 1800s, it has survived as a formal religion, but only 1 percent of Japanese currently identify as Christian. Many Japanese, however, are fascinated with the exotic rituals and symbols of Christian beliefs and ceremonies, even if they do not understand their religious meaning. Western Christian-style weddings are considered very trendy.

In 1996 Hideaki Anno's hit anime series *Neon Genesis Evangelion* incorporated various symbols and imagery from both Christianity and Judaism. The story takes place in the early twenty-first century when Earth is under attack by unknown magical aliens from space. Referred to as angels, their arrival has been prophesied by a bizarre interpretation of the Dead Sea Scrolls (ancient Jewish manuscripts) and the New Testament's book of Revelation. As the apocalyptic end of the world nears, humans fight back with giant robots.

Whether these themes and symbols were meant to convey serious religious ideas has long been debated by fans. In an interview, animator Kazuya Tsurumaki denies any such intent, stating, "There is no actual Christian meaning to the show, we just thought the visual symbols of Christianity look cool. If we had known the show would get distributed in the U.S. and Europe we might have rethought that choice."

Quoted in Owen Thomas, "Amusing Himself to Death: Kazuya Tsurumaki Speaks About the Logic and Illogic That Went into Creating FLCL," Eva Monkey, October 17, 2001. www.evamonkey.com.

typical cats, dragons, or birds, but Louise produces a real teenaged boy from Japan. Despite their odd partnership, together they help save the kingdom.

A more seriously odd pairing appears in the dark-magical "beauty and the beast" manga and anime series *The Ancient Magus' Bride*. The manga creator, Kore Yamazaki, did a massive amount of research into Celtic and British folklore, magic, and alchemy to create its historic setting and details. In the story, Chise Hatori, a Japanese teen, was orphaned when her father abandoned the family and her mother committed suicide. Shunned because of her ability to see supernatural beings, she feels alone and worthless, so she sells herself into slavery at a magical auction. She is bought by Elias Ainsworth, a mysterious and emotionless humanoid sorcerer with an animal skull and horns for a head, who intends to train her as his apprentice and make her his bride. Both are emotionally scarred, but they help each other heal. Because this story takes place outside of modern Japan in space and time, the historical and magical setting provides a fictional safe place for Japanese teens to learn about difficult issues such as depression and suicide. These types of issues are not usually discussed openly within modern Japanese families or society.

> ### FAST FACT
> Most Japanese are both Shinto and Buddhist, without being strong believers in either religion. Babies are typically blessed at a Shinto shrine. Many hold Western-style weddings. Most have traditional Buddhist funerals when they die.

MAGICAL GIRL POWER

Many popular anime feature magical girls who start out as normal teens and gain magical powers in exchange for a pledge to use them for good. Other common elements include cute animal familiars and a flashy scene in which the girls transform into their magical alter egos. *Cardcaptor Sakura* is a magical girl manga series and anime about a ten-year-old who accidentally releases magical cards from a book. The magical guardian of the cards, a cute animal named Keroberos, becomes her guide as she uses her newfound powers to recover the cards.

While most magical girl shows are fun and entertaining, they also carry important cultural messages about girl power and how it can be creatively expressed within Japanese society. Japanese culture is founded on traditional gender roles, which have historically restricted women and girls to homemaking and family life. The most famous magical girl show is *Sailor Moon*. This story centers on a normal (if lazy) Tokyo schoolgirl named Usagi Tsukino. To her surprise, she discovers that she is the reincarnated Princess of the Moon who can transform into the magical hero Sailor Moon. Soon she is joined by other schoolgirls who also transform into hero forms: Sailor Venus, Sailor Mercury, and so on. Together they have battles and adventures to defeat the dark powers. Over time, Usagi slowly transforms from a weak and frightened crybaby into a strong leader of the Sailor Guardians, offering a powerful role model for young Japanese women to follow.

Not all magical girl stories are as uplifting as *Sailor Moon*. *Madoka Magica* explores the dark side of magical girls. When school-

Japanese society tends toward traditional gender roles that restrict women and girls to homemaking and family life. Magical girl anime such as Sailor Moon *(pictured) show girls and young women exercising power and initiative.*

WITCHES AND MAGICAL GIRLS

Witches and magical girls in anime and manga were inspired by the TV series *Bewitched*, which aired in the United States from 1964 to 1972. As Japanese scholar Kumiko Saito explains, "The 1960s 'witch' housewife theme waned quickly in the United States, but various cultural symbolisms of magic smoothly translated into the Japanese climate, leading to Japan's four-decade-long obsession with the magical girl." *Sally the Witch*, the first magical girl anime, was released in 1966, followed in 1969 by *Akko-chan*. Both series focused on a single cute girl with magical powers in domestic adventures. Later shows such as *Sailor Moon* and the *PreCure* franchise focused on groups of magical girls working together to fight larger evil forces. Usually, the magical girl has a magical animal companion, or familiar, that serves as her adviser and a magical object (such as a gem) that transforms her from a normal girl into a magical girl. In most Western cartoons, witch characters are wicked or evil, but anime's magical girls are generally forces for good.

Kumiko Saito, "Magic, Shōjo, and Metamorphosis: Magical Girl Anime and the Challenges of Changing Gender Identities in Japanese Society," *Journal of Asian Studies*, February 2014, p. 148.

girl Madoka encounters a strange creature named Kyubey, the creature offers to make a contract with her. In exchange for granting a wish, Kyubey will transform her into a magical girl. At first, Madoka hesitates, but her friends accept the offer and they begin fighting evil witches who bring despair into the world. They then discover that magical girls have only two fates: they must either be killed in battles with witches or succumb to despair and turn into witches themselves, only to be killed by the next set of magical girls. Through these endless cycles, cosmic familiars like Kyubey harvest the emotional power of the magical girls and witches as their energy source. This grim anime fairy tale encourages viewers to think about the moral of the story: how may societies exploit the positive energy and optimism of the younger generation? How can teens avoid falling victim to others' expectations?

TRADITIONAL RELIGIOUS AND SPIRITUAL BELIEFS

Serious themes can also be found in anime and manga inspired by religion. Japan's two main religious traditions are Shinto and Buddhism. Shinto beliefs center on reverence for one's ancestors, the natural world, and the spirits (kami) in everything that exists. Over eighty thousand Shinto shrines are scattered across Japan. Buddhism, founded in India twenty-five hundred years ago, is a religious philosophy that teaches acceptance of life's impermanence, nonattachment to material needs and things, and the seeking of wisdom through meditation and spiritual and physical good works. Most Japanese people today practice some aspects of one or both of these traditions, often through rituals, customs, and festivals.

Some manga and anime reflect serious aspects of Buddhism and Shinto. Osamu Tezuka's eight-volume manga, *Buddha*, has sold over 20 million copies. Following the life and spiritual journey of Siddhartha Gautama, the founder of Buddhism, the series introduces his ideas to young adults and is often used as a teaching text in temples.

Based on Shinto philosophy, *Mushi-Shi* is an atmospheric, genre-busting, mythic mystery-horror series. It features Gingko, a curious young man who studies *mushi* (forms of life energy) to restore balance between the mushis' world and humans. In one episode, Gingko treats a boy infected with mushi that make him highly sensitive to sound. In another, invisible mushi cause a deadly pandemic. Although mushi are described as magical, Gingko's investigations are logical, medical, and scientific. Ultimately, he learns that mushi are essential life forces that deserve respect.

The Japanese cultural mix of Shinto and Buddhist ideas shows clearly in Miyazaki's *Spirited Away*. Regularly cited as one of the best films of all time, this visually rich and disturbing fantasy takes place in a complex spirit world. This world combines characters and elements from all areas of Japanese folklore, magic, and religious and spiritual beliefs. As Susan Napier writes, when

FAST FACT

In Shinto tradition, families and friends visit shrines on New Year's Day to bring good fortune for the rest of the year. Dozens of anime series—including *Kimi ni Todoke, Miss Kobayashi's Dragon Maid, Cardcaptor Sakura*, and even *Pokémon*—feature New Year's Day shrine visits.

A visually rich mix of imagination, folklore, magic, and religious and spiritual beliefs are at play in Hayao Miyazaki's Spirited Away. *Throughout the film, Chihiro (pictured on the right) encounters an array of spirits, witches, and gods.*

Chihiro realizes that her parents' "own greed and irresponsibility . . . have turned [them] into enormous pigs,"[11] she must redeem them by working in the magical bathhouse for the gods. There she overcomes many challenges as she serves a strange brew of spirits, witches, and Shinto river gods all with different powers, wants, and needs. Like the Buddha, Chihiro learns from her experiences, and through her good works, she earns a respected place in society and figures out for herself what to believe and value.

Spiritual and religious ideas play central roles in all cultures' storytelling. It is not surprising to find such themes reflected in anime and manga. As we grow up, all of us wonder who we are and where we fit into the grand scheme of the universe. Anime and manga provide American audiences with a chance to see how Japanese individuals and society have posed similar questions and tried to figure out the answers.

CHAPTER FIVE

NATURE AND SCIENCE

Japan is well known for the beauty of snow-capped Mount Fuji, delicate cherry blossoms, and exquisite gardens. It is also famous for earthquakes, typhoons, and tsunamis. Perhaps because of these contrasts, Japanese culture has great respect for the power of nature. Humans and all living things depend on nature for existence. Scientific knowledge helps us understand the amazing wonders and the terrific energy of the natural world. Many anime are inspired by nature's beauty and its complexity.

NATURAL BEAUTY

For hundreds of years, Japan has celebrated the arrival of spring with April's famous cherry blossom festivals, outdoor parties, and picnics. Since the blooms on cherry trees last only days, they represent an important idea in Japanese culture: *mono no aware* ("deep feeling about things"). This refers to the bittersweet emotions people feel as they realize that nothing lasts forever. Anime express this concept in scenes of natural beauty that appear then quickly disappear, reminding us of both the fragility of life and hope for its renewal.

Many such scenes appear in *My Neighbor Totoro*, where wild green meadows and gentle sunlight create peaceful rural moments common in Japan in the early twentieth century. Jap-

42

anese audiences feel nostalgia for those simpler times, when everyone believed in magical nature spirits (like Totoro) that only children could see. In such places, Japanese scholar Kosuke Fujiki explains, the two children "gain spiritual comfort and healing through their encounters with nature and its nonhuman inhabitants."[12]

NATURAL DISASTERS

Nature can comfort, but it can also present hazards and dangers. Located in one of the most active volcanic regions of the world, the islands of Japan are frequently shaken by earthquakes. On March 11, 2011, a magnitude 9.0 quake struck, sending a tsunami crashing into northern Japan. The destruction was widespread. Over 20,000 people died, and 250,000 people were forced to relocate. The tsunami also damaged the Fukushima Daiichi Nuclear Power Plant, causing radioactive contamination. The damage to the power plant forced the entire country to reduce power usage for years.

Such natural disasters leave physical and psychological scars, but such events also inspire creativity. Makoto Shinkai has written and directed three hit anime films that reflect on Japanese experiences with earthquakes. In *Your Name*, a large meteor strike symbolizes an earthquake as two teens try to evacuate their small town before it is destroyed. In *Weathering with You*, heavy rains and the flooding of climate change represent the aftermath of an earthquake. In this film, two teens find that the girl, Hina, is a Shinto weather maiden with special powers. If she stays in this world, she will cause more rain, so she must choose whether to leave her life and relationship or stay and doom Tokyo to eternal flooding.

Suzume deals with the 2011 earthquake directly. The title character is a high school girl who survived the tsunami but lost her

> ### FAST FACT
> Non-Japanese fans watching *Summer Wars* were confused about why the rogue computer program was called "love machine." It was an artificial intelligence program (known as AI in English). But in Japanese, *ai* means "love." The clever Japanese programmer made a pun that Japanese viewers understood while American audiences did not.

mother. When she meets college student Souta, she learns that earthquakes and natural disasters are caused by a giant supernatural worm that lives underground that both she and Souta can see. Since the worm emerges through open doors in abandoned places, the two begin a road trip to close these doors and prevent future disasters. To do so, they channel the emotions of the people who were once there and chant a Shinto-style prayer. When they end up in Suzume's hometown, they realize that the purpose of the trip was to heal her psychological trauma from the earthquake and the death of her mother. When asked about the film's meaning, Shinkai said, "I think some good can come from coexisting with earthquakes and the idea that our lives can be upended in an instant. That can bring melancholy, but it can also drive us to offer help to others and show more compassion or empathy to those affected, because it may not be us hit by a disaster now, but tomorrow, it could be."[13]

Earthquakes have impacted Japan's past, and they threaten its future. Several anime remind audiences of the important lessons to be learned from those frequent events. In *The Wind Rises*, Hayao Miyazaki depicts the harrowing moments when the

The earthquake and tsunami that struck Japan in 2011 caused widespread death and destruction (pictured). Natural disasters like these leave physical and psychological scars, but such events have also inspired creativity.

GIANT ROBOTS, AKA MECHA

Giant robot, or mecha (adapted from "mechanical"), anime are one of the most popular genres. The earliest mecha anime, *Gigantor* (1963) and manga *Giant Robo* (1967), were both created by Mitsuteru Yokoyama. They feature a young boy who works with a giant robot and controls it either by remote control or voice commands. *Tranzor Z* (1972) introduced the idea of a person piloting a robot from inside, now an almost universal mecha trope. In *Getter Robo* (1974), the robots change form, a concept that premiered in the United States in *Transformers* (1984). *Mobile Suit Gundam* (1979) spawned a franchise that continues to this day, with political stories of battles between various governments on Earth and in space. *Neon Genesis Evangelion* (1996) was a groundbreaking mecha series that looked at the dark and real psychological trauma that would result if teenagers controlled giant weapons. These stories may be so popular because they are empowerment fantasies that feature a young child or teen who gains great power by piloting a robot. Since adolescents often feel helpless against the adult world, this theme makes these stories very appealing.

Great Kantō Earthquake of 1923 destroyed much of Tokyo. He shows how countless lives were lost and knocked off course by the disaster. To offer hope, he highlights the many acts of kindness that helped people survive and recover. In Masaaki Yuasa's anime series *Japan Sinks: 2020*, the fictional aftermath of a massive earthquake causes most of Japan to sink into the ocean. Through this what-if scenario, viewers imagine how they might endure personal losses, but they also ponder: What do they value most about their culture? What would they save?

In Miyazaki's *Ponyo*, a typhoon and tsunami place children in peril. Five-year-old Sōsuke and the fish-girl Ponyo must care for each other through weather-related and emotional storms, both partially caused by their parents' poor choices. Inspired by Shakespeare's storm-survivor play *The Tempest*, as Susan Napier notes, "Ponyo's vision of a restored natural order in which children will lead us to a purer, kinder world offers hope for a better future."[14]

HUMANITY VERSUS NATURE?

Humanity's growing population and industrial development have caused negative effects on our planet and many unintended consequences. As an island nation with limited natural resources,

FAST FACT

In a Japanese folktale, a fisherman visits the undersea dragon's palace (Ryūgū-jō) and returns with a magical box. In the 2010s the Japanese space agency sent a spacecraft to an asteroid to bring back a container of rocks, so they named the asteroid Ryugu after the dragon's palace.

Japan has a long history of environmental awareness. Important manga and anime provide serious perspectives on such issues. Most famous is Miyazaki's postapocalyptic epic, *Nausicaä of the Valley of the Wind*. In this story, humanity is dying out, and most of the world is covered by poisonous forests inhabited by giant insects. Most believe that humans' only hope is to destroy the insects and reclaim the land, but as Nausicaä learns through her botanical studies, humans have it all wrong. The supposedly toxic plants are actually cleansing the pollution caused by previous generations, not causing it. By teaching people to work with the forest, she restores some balance to humanity's relationship with nature. This film ends with one of Miyazaki's most powerful visual images: a small green plant emerges from the purified sand near the discarded gas mask that Nausicaä no longer needs.

As an island nation with limited natural resources, Japan has a long history of environmental awareness. This awareness is reflected in anime such as Nausicaä of the Valley of the Wind, *in which the title character must investigate and solve the mystery behind the earth's extensive pollution.*

DARK SCIENCE

While scientific studies of nature can help people live in better balance with it, science and technology also have dark sides. During World War II, the United States developed the first atomic bombs and dropped two of them—one on Hiroshima and one on Nagasaki—ending the war with Japan. Over one hundred thousand people were killed and ninety thousand injured. As the only country to have these horrific weapons used against it, Japanese culture is still trying to make sense of these events. In *Barefoot Gen*, a partially autobiographical manga, Keiji Nakazawa relates the story of six-year-old Gen Nakaoka, whose family lived near Hiroshima at the time of the bombing. After losing his father and younger brother, Gen witnesses the struggles of fellow survivors through the days and years ahead. Originally published in Japan from 1973 to 1987, this emotionally touching manga was one of the first to be translated and published in the United States. The trauma caused by this war still affects later generations of Japanese. Fumiyo Kōno's manga *In This Corner of the World* (2007–2009) relates how Suzu, a young wife and budding artist, loses her right hand in the Hiroshima bombing but gradually regains her spirit to build a new creative life. Through such stories, Japanese audiences learn valuable lessons of resilience and strength.

SPACE SCIENCE AND FUTURISTIC PHYSICS

Like other folks worldwide, the Japanese eagerly follow their country's space program and love the idea of space travel and exploration. Anime and manga reflect this obsession. One classic space series is Leiji Matsumoto's dreamlike *Galaxy Express 999*. Inspired by Miyazawa's *Night on the Galactic Railroad*, this long saga follows Tetsuro Hoshino as he travels from Earth to the Andromeda Galaxy to get a mechanical body that will allow him to live forever. As he learns, immortality will not solve his problems, so he returns to Earth. A fan favorite, *Cowboy Bebop*, combines fun science fiction themes with westerns, crime

> **FAST FACT**
>
> When images of atomic fireballs appear in anime, they carry serious messages. *Akira* takes place after fictional Tokyo is destroyed by a surprise atomic bomb and rebuilt as Neo-Tokyo. The movie ends when Neo-Tokyo itself is destroyed with another apocalyptic explosion to symbolize how the cycle of violence mindlessly repeats itself.

drama, and a jazz soundtrack to create an action-adventure about a trio of eccentric bounty hunters who travel through the twenty-first-century solar system.

Other space-science-themed anime aim for more technical accuracy. The *Planetes* series, set in 2075, is based on the real problem of space junk, all the small satellites and debris in low Earth orbit that now create hazards for other spacecraft. Combining humor with drama, this story follows a group of international blue-collar astronauts (mostly Japanese) on their thankless job cleaning up space trash.

As in recent live-action films, the futuristic idea of the multiverse appears in anime too. Makoto Shinkai's *The Place Promised in Our Early Days* is set in an alternate modern Japan, where Russia and the United States divide up the country after World War II. The scientists in this alternate reality build machines to establish contact with other worlds in the multiverse. As with other science fiction works, Shinkai's adventure draws his audience's attention to a real-life dilemma: Japanese society often finds itself caught between larger economic and geopolitical powers.

LIVING WITH NATURE

More down-to-earth anime offer fresh perspectives on humanity's relationship with nature. In Japan the subject of climate change has long been taught in schools, so many young adults have grown up understanding the environmental crisis. Japanese teens often wonder what they can do to help.

One good place to start is to appreciate that humans are always truly part of the natural world, not separate from it. In *Moyasimon: Tales of Agriculture*, Tadayasu Sawaki grows up on his family's farm. Able to see and communicate with microor-

ARTIFICIAL INTELLIGENCE

Japan is a world leader in electronics and robotics, so themes about the pros and cons of artificial intelligence have long appeared in manga and anime. Osamu Tezuka's *Astro Boy* relates the story of a robot boy (Atom) with superpowers and human emotions. As Frederik L. Schodt notes, "Unlike American superheroes that usually fought for justice, [Astro Boy] also fought for the ultimate goal of postwar Japan—peace." The film *Ghost in the Shell* posits a dark future in which everyone is continually plugged in to the virtual world and the line between reality and cyberspace is disappearing. Major Motoko Kusanagi, a cyborg special agent fighting a cybercriminal known only as the Puppet Master, discovers that it is not a human but a rogue computer program that has escaped into the computer networks. In *Sing a Bit of Harmony*, transfer student Shion Ashimori turns out to be an android. She is part of an experiment to improve how AIs interact with humans. Rather than wanting to dominate and destroy the world, Shion's goal is to bring happiness and joy to humans through music.

Frederik L. Schodt, *The Astro Boy Essays: Osamu Tezuka, Mighty Atom, Manga/Anime Revolution*. Berkeley, CA: Stone Bridge, 2007, p. 4.

ganisms since childhood, he later applies his ability at agricultural college. In the series, bacteria, mold, and fungus all appear as comic characters who explain their roles in ecosystems, farming, and the fermentation of alcohol and food. As this anime shows, all living things—humans included—can help sustain the cycle of life.

Ayumu Watanabe's *Children of the Sea* offers a complex and fascinating tale inspired by this generation's challenge to understand nature and save our planet. Other anime remind us that we do not need PhDs to learn about and love nature. Japanese culture has long recognized the emotional and physical healing value of "forest bathing" (*shinrin yoku*); that is, spending quiet time calmly appreciating natural spaces. In *Laid-Back Camp*, high school girls form an Outdoor Exploration Club and enjoy camping adventures in beautiful natural places. In *A Place Further than the Universe*, four Japanese high school girls join an expedition to Antarctica.

As these intriguing anime and manga teach us, there are always new worlds to explore. Discovering the awesome wonder of natural places can help us find hope on the horizon.

CHAPTER SIX

DAILY LIFE AND CULTURE

Culture does not just refer to a society's major creative achievements in history, art, literature, religion, and science. Most folks experience their national culture as a big accumulation of all the little things that go into living life, such as food, clothing, family traditions, school routines and expectations, work, social rules and customs, festivals, and holidays. Part of the fun of enjoying anime and manga comes from the peek they give us into Japanese lifeways: bento boxes, rice balls, slurping noodles, indoor shoes, shoji screens, crazytiny apartments, school uniforms and grade hierarchies, cat cafés, convenience stores, and crowded Tokyo intersections.

Anime and manga stories also give audiences insight into the inner lives of Japanese people and the social relationships and personal choices that form the culture they collectively create. Individuals may have a common sense of being Japanese, but they experience their social and personal identities in diverse ways.

YOUNG ADULT CULTURE AND SCHOOL

Teens and young adults are the primary market for manga and anime in Japan, so characters are often the same age and are shown dealing with similar life situations, especially school. Whether realistic or fantasy, school storylines typically concern friends and romances, home-work and grades, helpful or antagonistic teachers, issues with student council, music, sports, cram school, and after-school clubs. One unique feature of Japanese high schools is that they vary in academic difficulty and specialties, so middle school students must pass application exams and apply for admission to specific ones. To improve their exam scores, students often attend cram school, which involves many

> **FAST FACT**
>
> On Valentine's Day in Japan, a girl gives chocolate to a boy she likes, hoping that he will give her chocolate one month later on White Day. Valentine anime episodes often feature characters trying to get their crush to notice them or agonizing over whether to give obligatory chocolate to guys or girls who are just friends.

hours of afterschool study sessions before they head home to start their regular homework. Once in high school, students face even more competition and more cram school to get into desirable, high-ranking colleges. While no series is entirely based on such issues, the stresses of academic life and the lack of down time appear as common plot elements.

Most Japanese high schools encourage after-school activities and allow students to create clubs based on their interests. In the extremely popular series, *K-On!*, four girls in an after-school light music club form a band and start performing. *K-On!* was one of the first anime to define a new subgenre: cute girls doing cute things. The anime soap opera *Sound! Euphonium* follows the central character, Kumiko Oumae, a first-year euphonium player, and her group of concert band friends as they struggle through high school. As the band attempts to win national competitions, their story of mutual support emphasizes traditional Japanese social values of striving to be one's best while working together to achieve common goals.

While school life presents many creative opportunities, it can also bring academic pressures, issues with interpersonal relationships, depression, and anxiety. Anime and manga engage such problems and offer possible solutions. In *Komi Can't Communicate*, Shouko Komi is seen by her classmates as the most beautiful and aloof girl in school, but actually she is terrified to speak and can only communicate by writing. When her classmate, Hitohito Tadano, who is on the bottom rung of the school's social ladder, discovers her secret, he sets out to help her achieve her dream of making one hundred friends.

Anywhere in the world it likely feels awkward to be the new kid in class, but in Japanese schools, social hierarchies and class rank can create immense tension between upper-grade and lower-grade students. Younger students are expected to show great respect to their seniors at all times, and sometimes the unequal power relationship can become emotionally or physically abusive. In Japan school bullying can continue into adult workplaces and neighborhoods. *A Silent Voice* deals with the story of Shoya Ishida, who led his elementary class in teasing and mocking a new deaf girl, Shoko Nishimiya. When this behavior escalated to the point that Shoya destroys her hearing aids, her family pulled her out of school. The class then turned on Shoya, making him the scapegoat for the behavior that they all participated in. Now in high school, he has fallen into depression and contemplates suicide but decides instead to find Shoko to try to make amends. Shoko accepts his offer of friendship, but this starts a

Bullying, which often begins in school and sometimes carries over into the workplace, is a topic of concern in Japan. A Silent Voice *(pictured) deals with the topic of bullying in schools.*

ANIME AND SOCIAL MEDIA

As in the United States, social media plays a major role in the lives of Japan's population, especially teens and young adults. So of course, social media is featured in anime. Two of Mamoru Hosoda's films deal directly with social media and its effects. In *Summer Wars*, the social media platform OZ serves as the interface for everything from online gaming to running municipal water systems. When a rogue AI program threatens to destroy OZ (and part of the real world with it), one family in Japan uses the tools of social media to stop it. In *Belle* an emotionally scarred young girl re-creates herself as the singing avatar Belle in the social media world of U. Despite the dangers social media presents, Hosoda views it optimistically, seeing it as a potential means of building positive communities for the users.

rocky series of events that leads to more issues between them and their families. As anime scholar Jonathan Clements writes, "*A Silent Voice* is a deliberately challenging work, repeatedly introducing stereotypical characters and situations, only to subvert and transform them with additional information. It deals not only with disability, but spousal abandonment, single parenthood, the integration of immigrants, suicide and most notably of all, bullying."[15]

RELATIONSHIPS AND SOCIAL LIFE

In Japan, as in all world cultures, society is based on networks of interpersonal relationships. Adolescence is a time to learn and develop emotional life skills that prepare young adults for their future family and work lives. Young romance narratives help readers and viewers navigate the drama of relationships and learn how to appreciate and care for others. Most *shōjo* (young girl) anime and manga are romances and romantic comedies. A classic example is *Whisper of the Heart*, which follows a young girl and aspiring writer named Shizuku Tsukishima. She falls in love with a boy named Seiji Amasawa, who is learning to craft violins. As the standard plotline unfolds, they start out as antagonists who slowly discover their true feelings for each other, then have their future threatened when Seiji gets a scholarship to spend a year studying violin making in Italy.

Young romance stories help readers and viewers navigate the drama of relationships and learn how to appreciate and care for others. Whisper of the Heart follows the evolving relationship between a girl who aspires to be a writer and a boy who is learning to craft violins.

A popular subgenre of romance is harem anime and manga, in which the main character is a boy surrounded by several girls, all of whom are possible romantic interests. (Stories about a girl surrounded by males are called reverse harem). Such narratives follow the dramatic and humorous "will they/won't they" tension that sometimes develops during adolescence when childhood platonic friendships start to become romantic relationships. One example is *We Never Learn*, in which a smart but impoverished high school boy Nariyuki Yuiga is hired to tutor three of his female classmates because college entrance exams are on the horizon. The three girls are Fumino Furuhashi, a literature genius wanting to study science in college; Rizu Ogata, a nerd science genius who cannot read social cues but wants to study the arts and psychology; and Uruka Takemoto, who is on the verge of getting an athletic scholarship to college but is failing all her academic courses. Through much struggling, Nariyuki manages to help all of them succeed academically, but not before teasing the audience with a possible romance with each of them.

> **FAST FACT**
> To get an edge on highly competitive college entrance exams, some high school students will take after-school classes at "cram schools," where they are drilled on the likely test material. The misery of cram school is a frequent theme in anime and manga.

Since so much of Japanese culture emphasizes the importance of blending in and conforming to social norms, a popular type of fantasy-romance anime considers when opposites attract—situations in which one person is extremely popular and outgoing while the other is shy, unpopular, or an outcast. In *My Dress-Up Darling*, Wakana Gojō is an introvert whose dream is to take over his grandfather's doll-making shop. One day after school, the loud and outgoing Marin Kitagawa discovers him using the home economics sewing machines to make doll clothing. Marin's passion is cosplay, the hobby where kids make costumes to role-play characters from anime or video games. Not being very good at sewing, she talks Wakana into helping her create her costumes. In spite of their obvious differences, they begin a tentative romance that pulls Wakana out of his shell. The series draws its popularity from both the "ugly duckling" story of Wakana and its fun references to the exciting world of cosplay fan culture.

PERSONAL BEHAVIOR AND IDENTITY

Expectations for proper behavior and gender identity present challenges that all adolescents face, and anime explores them through comedy and drama. *Ranma ½* is the classic comic gender-swap manga and anime series. The title character, Ranma Saotome, is a teenage boy and martial artist in training who is living under a curse. When splashed with cold water, he turns into a girl, while hot water returns him to being a boy. While the macho Ranma is highly annoyed at first with this curse, by the end of the series he discovers that there are a lot of situations in which being a girl is actually advantageous. As Susan Napier describes the story, "At the personal level, the viewer watches the appealing characters . . . as they attempt to construct their gender identities while navigating the confusing tides of adolescence. At the public level, the series shows the gender norms that society attempts to impose upon them through the agencies of school and family."[16]

In the *Tomo-chan Is a Girl!* series, a pair of students who have been buddies since elementary school, Junichiro Kubota and tomboy Tomo Aizawa, navigate changes to their personal identities and their relationship as they go through puberty. Now that they are in high school, Tomo is still a tomboy but has developed a major crush on Junichiro, who still sees her as just one of the guys. The comedy arises from the interplay of Tomo's clumsy attempts to fit into gender normative behavior and Junichiro being a typical clueless male.

HOW REALISTIC ARE ANIME HIGH SCHOOLS?

Do students in Japan really meet secretly or hide out on school rooftops at lunch? Do student council members really rule their schools? Do students really live alone in their own apartments while still attending high school? These are common anime tropes—recurring images used to express important themes.

In the real world, some older schools in Japan do allow access to the roof, but nowadays most keep them locked and off limits. Likewise, while many anime present the student council as the rulers of the school, in reality the teachers and administrators are the real authorities. And almost no high school student lives alone in an apartment while attending school. If they do go to another city to attend school, they usually live in a dormitory, at a group house, or with relatives.

On the other hand, some things you see in anime high schools are real. There are shoe lockers near the entrance, and all students wear indoor slippers called *uwabaki* while at school. When watching anime, be careful not to assume that because something happens on-screen, that's how things really are in Japan. Not all teenaged Japanese boys are secretly mecha pilots, and not all teenaged Japanese girls are shrine maidens with magical powers.

A more thoughtful approach to gender identity issues appears in the manga and anime series *Wandering Son*. The story opens as fifth grader Shuichi Nitori, a feminine student assigned male at birth, befriends Yoshino Takatsuki, a tomboy who wants to be a boy. The two bond over their shared desire to switch genders, and the rest of the series follows their growing friendship through several grades as they navigate the attitudes and reactions of their parents, teachers, and classmates, face their own questions of identity, and deal with puberty. Attitudes toward gender identity and roles are still as uncertain in Japanese society as they are in current American society, but this series excels in presenting a sympathetic view of all involved. Because of its literary quality and sensitivity, the manga series was recommended by both the Japan Media Arts Festival in 2006 and the American Library Association's Young Adult Library Services Association in 2012.

Young adult audiences in the United States may instantly identify with many aspects of teen life and culture represented in anime and manga. Yet it is important to remember that every national culture is made up of diverse subcultures that may present unique concerns, challenges, and references whose meanings may not be obvious to outside observers. By carefully learning from such stories, though, we can improve our understanding of other cultures and develop new perspectives on how others' lives matter.

SOURCE NOTES

INTRODUCTION: CROSS-CULTURAL UNDERSTANDING VERSUS MISUNDERSTANDING

1. Justin Chang, "Review: 'Belle' Is a Striking Virtual Reality Riff on 'Beauty and the Beast,'" *Los Angeles Times*, January 13, 2022. www.latimes.com.

CHAPTER ONE: ART AND OTHER FORMS OF VISUAL STORYTELLING

2. Frederik L. Schodt, *Manga! Manga! The World of Japanese Comics*. Tokyo: Kodansha International, 1983, p. 28.
3. Helen McCarthy, *The Art of Osamu Tezuka: God of Manga*. New York: Abrams, 2009, p. 8.
4. Kayson Carlin, "The Crossover of Anime and Japanese Theatre," NEET Knowledge Base, February 10, 2019. https://neetknowledgebase.wordpress.com.

CHAPTER TWO: HISTORICAL ERAS AND EVENTS

5. Schodt, *Manga! Manga!*, p. 17.
6. Susan Napier, *Miyazakiworld: A Life in Art*. New Haven, CT: Yale University Press, 2018, p. 118.
7. Antonia Levi, *Samurai from Outer Space: Understanding Japanese Animation*. Chicago: Open Court, 2001, p. 35.

CHAPTER THREE: LITERATURE

8. Quoted in Daisuke Akimoto, "Learning Peace and Coexistence with Nature Through Animation: *Nausicaä of the Valley of the Wind*," *Ritsumeikan Journal of Asia Pacific Studies*, 2014, p. 54.
9. Quoted in Marc Hairston and Nobutoshi Ito, "Interview with Yoshitoshi ABe," *Animerica*, September 2003, pp. 45, 47.
10. Roland Kelts, *Japanamerica: How Japanese Pop Culture Has Invaded the U.S.* New York: St. Martin's Griffin, 2007, p. 42.

CHAPTER FOUR: FOLKLORE, MAGIC, AND RELIGIOUS AND SPIRITUAL BELIEFS

11. Susan Napier, *Anime from* Akira *to* Howl's Moving Castle*: Experiencing Contemporary Japanese Animation*. New York: Palgrave, 2005, p. 182.

CHAPTER FIVE: NATURE AND SCIENCE

12. Kosuke Fujiki, "*My Neighbor Totoro*: The Healing of Nature, the Nature of Healing," *Resilience: A Journal of the Environmental Humanities*, 2015, p. 153.
13. Quoted in Jeremy Fuster, "Why Makoto Shinkai Made a Talking Chair the Heart of 'Suzume,'" The Wrap, April 14, 2023. www.thewrap.com.
14. Napier, *Miyazakiworld*, p. 244.

CHAPTER SIX: DAILY LIFE AND CULTURE

15. Jonathan Clements, "Enemies Reunited," *All the Anime* (blog), May 18, 2017. https://blog.alltheanime.com.
16. Napier, *Anime from* Akira *to* Howl's Moving Castle, p. 53.

FOR FURTHER RESEARCH

BOOKS

Jonathan Clements, *Anime: A History*. London: Bloomsbury, 2023.

Jonathan Clements, *A Brief History of Japan: Samurai, Shogun and Zen: The Extraordinary Story of the Land of the Rising Sun*. Tokyo: Tuttle, 2017.

Jonathan Clements and Helen McCarthy, *The Anime Encyclopedia: A Century of Japanese Animation*, 3rd rev. ed. Berkeley, CA: Stone Bridge, 2015.

Alex Dudok de Wit, *Grave of the Fireflies*. London: Bloomsbury, 2021.

Roland Kelts, *Japanamerica: How Japanese Pop Culture Has Invaded the U.S.* New York: St. Martin's Griffin, 2007.

Helen McCarthy, *The Art of Osamu Tezuka, God of Manga*. New York: Abrams, 2009.

Helen McCarthy, *500 Essential Anime Movies*. New York: Collins Design, 2008.

Susan Napier, *Miyazakiworld: A Life in Art*. New Haven, CT: Yale University Press, 2018.

Andrew Osmond, *Spirited Away*, 2nd ed. London: Bloomsbury, 2020.

Deborah Scally, *Miyazaki and the Hero's Journey*. Jefferson, NC: McFarland, 2022.

Frederik L. Schodt, *Manga! Manga! The World of Japanese Comics*. Tokyo: Kodansha International, 2013.

JOURNALS

Mechademia
www.mechademia.net/journal
Mechademia is an academic journal of scholarly articles about anime, manga, and fan culture.

Resilience: A Journal of the Environmental Humanities
www.resiliencejournal.org/past-issues/issue-2-3
This issue of the journal features multiple accessible essays on manga and anime.

INTERNET SOURCES

Sam Anderson, "Spirited Away to Miyazaki Land," *New York Times*, February 14, 2023. www.nytimes.com.

Ligaya Mishan, "Hayao Miyazaki Prepares to Cast One Last Spell," *New York Times*, November 21, 2021. www.nytimes.com.

Maya Phillips, "The Power of Hugs in Anime," *New York Times*, August 11, 2022. www.nytimes.com.

Charles Solomon, "For the Most Complex Heroines in Animation, Look to Japan," *New York Times*, June 24, 2022. www.nytimes.com.

WEBSITES

All the Anime
https://blog.alltheanime.com
This site includes short reviews and essays about current anime films and series along with short pieces about key figures in the history of anime production.

Anime News Network
www.animenewsnetwork.com
This is a popular online news source for anime, manga, and video games. In addition to news, it provides reviews, press releases, and anime convention reports.

History of Japan, Japan-Guide.com
www.japan-guide.com/e/e641.html
This Japan travel website includes a good overview of the periods in Japanese history and key elements of Japanese culture, including important emperors and castles.

Sora News 24
https://soranews24.com
This English-language website covers some of the same anime news as *Anime News Network*, but also covers other aspects of Japanese and Asian popular culture such as Asia-specific foods, Asian fashions, and silly news items like Japanese KFCs dressing up their Col. Sanders mannequins as samurai.

ANIME AND MANGA WORTH EXPLORING

The Ancient Magus' Bride
Belle
Ghost in the Shell
The Girl Who Leapt Through Time
Grave of the Fireflies
Haibane-Renmei
In This Corner of the World
Madoka Magica
The Melancholy of Haruhi Suzumiya
Metropolis
Millennium Actress
Miss Hokusai
Mushi-Shi
My Neighbor Totoro
Nadia: The Secret of Blue Water
Nausicaä of the Valley of the Wind
Neon Genesis Evangelion
Night on the Galactic Railroad
Patema Inverted
Princess Mononoke
Ranma ½
Revolutionary Girl Utena
A Silent Voice
Spirited Away
Summer Wars
Suzume
The Tale of the Princess Kaguya
Violet Evergarden
Wolf Children
Your Name

INDEX

Note: Boldface page numbers indicate illustrations.

ABe, Yoshitoshi, 30–31
Akko-cha (magical girl anime), 39
akuma (demons), 33
Alakazam the Great (anime), 26
Amaterasu (sun goddess), **17**, 17–18, 22
Ancient Magus' Bride, The (manga/anime series), 37
anime
   influences on, 12–13, 31–32
   numbers created, 5
   origins of, 14
   social media and, 53
   space-science-themed, 47–48
   theatrical productions of, 15
Anno, Hideaki, 32, 36
artificial intelligence (AI), 49
Asagiri, Kafka, 30
Astro Boy (TV anime show), 14, **15**, 49

Bakuman (anime), 9
Barefoot Gen (manga), 47
Belle (anime), 6–7
Bishop Toba Scrolls, 8–9
Bleach (anime series), 27
Buddha (manga series), 40
Buddhism, 20, 25, 37, 39, 40
Bungo Stray Dogs (anime/manga series), 30
Bunraku (puppet theater), 9

Cardcaptor Sakura (manga/anime series), 37
caricature cartoons, 13
Carlin, Kayson, 15
Castle in the Sky (anime film), **31**, 31–32
Chang, Justin, 7

Children of the Sea (anime film), 49
Clements, Jonathan, 14, 53
cosplay, 55
Cowboy Bebop (anime film), 47–48
cram schools, 55
creation myths, 17–18

Dagger of Kamui, The (anime series), 19
Dead Sea Scrolls, 36
Demon Slayer (anime/manga series), 34, **35**
denki kamishibai (electric kamishibai), 11
De Wit, Alex Dudok, 28
doors, Shinto and representation of, 5
Dragonball (anime series), 26

Fairy Tail (anime series), 27
Familiar of Zero, The (anime series), 36
familiars (animal companions), 36–37, 39
Fujiki, Kosuke, 43
Fukushima Daiichi Nuclear Power Plant disaster, 43

Galaxy Express 999 (anime film), 47
Gankutsuou (anime), 32
Gautama, Siddhartha, 40
gender identity, 55–57
Girl Who Leapt Through Time, The (anime film), 28–29
"Grave of the Fireflies" (Akiyuki Nosaka), 28
Great Wave off Kanagawa, The (Hokusai), 12, **12**, 14

Haibane-Renmei (TV anime series), 30–31
Hard-Boiled Wonderland and the End of the World (Haruki Murakami), 30–31
harem anime/manga, 54–55

high schools, anime, 56
Hokusai, Katsushika, 11–12, 14
Homer, 27
Hosoda, Mamoru, 6, 29, 53
How Do You Live? (Yoshino), 30
Howl's Moving Castle (anime film), 32, 35

impressionist movement, 12–13
In This Corner of the World (manga), 47
Inu-Oh (anime), 9, **10**, 21

Japan
   celebration of natural beauty in, 42–43
   classical era, 20–21
   early era, 17–19
   introduction of Christianity in, 36
   main time periods of, 16
   modern era, 22–24
   natural disasters in, 43–45
   religious/spiritual beliefs of, 39–41
Japanese culture, 7
   relationships/social life, 53–55
   young adult/school, 50–53
Japanese myths, 17–18
Japan Sinks: 2020 (anime series), 45
Journey to the West (*The Monkey King*, anime), 25, 26

Kabuki theater, 9–11
kami (souls, divine spirits), 5, 22, 40
kamishibai (paper play), 11
Katsushika, Oi, 14
Kelts, Roland, 32
Kimba the White Lion (anime), 14
Kon, Satoshi, 24

63

Kōno, Fumiyo, 47
Kubrick, Stanley, 14

Laid-Back Camp (anime film), 49
Legend of the White Serpent (anime film), 25
Levi, Antonia, 19
Life of Budori Gusuko, The (anime), 23, **23**
Little Witch Academia (anime film), 35–36

Madoka Magica (magical girl anime), 38–39
magical girls, 37–39
manga
  influences on, 12–13, 31–32
  as new variation of ancient storytelling, 8
  numbers published, 5
  origins of, 13
  theatrical productions of, 15
Matsumoto, Leiji, 47
McCarthy, Helen, 13
mecha anime, 19, 45
Melancholy of Haruhi Suzumiya, The (anime series), 34
Metropolis (manga), 18
mie (freeze-frame pose), 10–11
Millennium Actress (anime film), 24
Miss Hokusai (anime film), 14
Miyazaki, Hayao, 18, 19, 30, 31, 35, 40, **41**, 44–45, 46
  on influence of Tezuka, 14
  on *Nausicaä*, 27
Miyazawa, Kenji, 23, 27, 30, 47
Möbius strip, 32
Moyasimon: Tales of Agriculture (anime film), 49
Murakami, Haruki, 30–31
Mushi Production, 14
Mushi-Shi (anime/manga series), 40
My Master Has No Tail (anime), 11
My Songuku (manga serial), 26

Nadia—the Secret of Blue Water (anime/manga series), 32

Napier, Susan, 40–41, 45, 56
Naruto (anime series), 27
natural disasters, 5, 43–45
Nausicaä of the Valley of the Wind (epic manga), 27, 46, **46**
Neon Genesis Evangelion (anime series), 36
Night on the Galactic Railroad (fantasy novella), 27–28, 47
Noh theater, 9, **10**
Nosaka, Akiyuki, 28

Odyssey, The (Homer), 27
One Piece (anime series), 27
oni (villains), 33
Otaku Elf (manga/anime series), 22
Our Home's Fox Deity (light novel, anime), 34

Paprika (science fiction novel, anime film), 29, **29**
pictograms, 8
Place Further than the Universe, A (anime film), 49
Place Promised in Our Early Days, The (anime film), 48
Planetes, The (anime series), 48
Pom Poko (anime), 34
Ponyo (anime film), 45

rakugo (visual storytelling), 11
Ranma 1/2 (manga/anime series), 55–56
Ranpo, Edogawa, 30
Rose of Versailles, The (stage production), 15
Royal Shakespeare Company, 13

Sailor Moon (magical girl anime series), 11, 18, 38, **38**, 39
  stage production of, 15
Saito, Kumiko, 39
samurai, 19
Samurai Champloo (TV anime series), 23–24
Samurai X (anime series), 19
Schodt, Frederik L., 9, 10, 49
science fiction, 27–29
Secret World of Arrietty, The (anime film), 32
Shinkai, Makoto, 4, 43, 44, 48
  themes used by, 5

Shinto, 5, 18, 22, 37, 39–40
Shirabako (anime), 9
Shōwa Genroku Rakugo Shinju (anime), 11
Silent Voice, A, **52**, 52–53
social media, 53
Son Goku (the Monkey King), 26
Sound! Euphonium (anime soap opera), 51
Spirited Away (anime film), 22, 40–41, **41**
spirits. *See* kami; yokai
Spring and Chaos (anime), 23
Summer Wars (anime film), 43, 53
Super Kabuki, 15
Suzuki, Toshio, 30
Suzume (anime film), 4–5, **6**, 43–44

Takahata, Isao, 13, 20–21, 28, 34
Takarazuka Revue, 15
Tale of the Princess Kaguya, The (anime), 13, 20–21
Tezuka, Osamu, 13–14, **15**, 26, 40, 49
Tiger in the Snow (anime film), 14
Toriyama, Akira, 26
tricksters, 34
Tsuchigumo (*yokai),* **35**
Tsurumaki, Kazuya, 36
Tsutsui, Yasutaka, 28–29

ukiyo-e (painting/printmaking style), 11–12
Urusei Yatsura (anime/manga series), 33

Watanabe, Ayumu, 49
Weathering with You (anime film), 43
We Never Learn (harem anime/manga), 54–55
witches/wizards, 35–37
Witch Hat Atelier (manga series), 36
World Masterpiece Theater (animated series), 32

Yamazaki, Kore, 37
yokai (spirits), 33, 34, 35
Yoshino, Genzaburo, 30
Your Name (anime film), 43
Yuasa, Masaaki, 9, 21, 45